Volume 5

BRITISH RAILWAYS IN COLOUR

Alan Earnshaw & Kevin Derrick

C000216838

SCOTTISH REGION

60024

Nostalgia Road Publications

The **British Railways In Colour** Series™

is produced under licence by

Nostalgia Road Publications Ltd.

Unit 6, Chancel Place

Shap Road Industrial Estate, Kendal LA9 6NZ

Tel. 01539 738832 - Fax: 01539 730075

designed and published by
Trans-Pennine Publishing Ltd.
PO Box 10,
Appleby-in-Westmorland,
Cumbria, CA16 6FA
Tel. 017683 51053 Fax. 017683 53558
e-mail: admin@transpenninepublishing.co.uk

and printed by
Kent Valley Colour Printers Ltd.
Kendal, Cumbria
01539 741344

© Trans-Pennine Publishing Ltd. 2004
Photographs: As credited

Front Cover: The charm of Scotland's railways are clearly found in this 1959 picture of 67474 at Garelochead. This push and pull-fitted 2-4-2T was one of just two survivors from the Reid North British Class of 1911. They were used on motor trains between Craigendoran and Arrochar in Argylshire.
Trans-Pennine Archive (E291)

Rear Cover Top: An up freight at Blairgowrie is in the capable hands of B1 Class 4-6-0 61347 from Thornton Junction MPD (62A) on one of those glorious sunny days on 23rd August 1966. *J. R. Beddows* (E268)

Rear Cover Bottom: Allocated to St. Rollox (65B), this BR Standard Class 5MT, 73152, has Caprotti valve gear. It is pictured at Glasgow's Buchanan Street Station in June 1965 - or around 18 months before the station shut its doors to passengers forever.
Strathwood Library Collection (B258)

Title Page: Here A4 Pacific 60024 *Kingfisher* shows its power on the up Grampian Express near Perth on 24th August 1967.
J.R. Beddows (E366)

This Page: One of the Scottish A2 Pacifics, 60527 *Sun Chariot* waits to set off from Glasgow Queen Street with a special at Easter 1964.
Richard Icke (E280)

ISBN 1 903016 33 9
British Cataloguing in Publication Data
A catalogue record for this book is available from the British Library

WELCOME to the fifth volume of the **British Railways in Colour** series, which deals with what has to be one of the least photographed of the British Railway regions, the Scottish. Created out of the LMS and LNER systems north of the border in 1948, the Scottish Region has to be considered one of the most charming of all the BR divisions.

From the industrial centres of the Clyde-Forth isthmus, to the remote and lonely branches to Mallaig and the Kyle of Lochalsh, the region was one of outstanding contrasts. Even in its rural areas, the railway lines differed greatly from the Highlands down to the Border counties. Sadly, many of these lines were not widely visited by colour photographers, and a wealth of railway heritage passed quietly into the pages of history.

Above: *Here we see a BR Standard 2-6-0 4MT 76004 as it pulls away from Glasgow Central on 1st August 1966. Although it was far from its projected 'life-expired' date, it was withdrawn from Polmadie MPD (66A) just two months later. It was unceremoniously scrapped at Campbells at Airdrie in January 1967.* Michael Beaton (B306)

The romance of Scottish steam is well-captured in the pages of this book, as it contains a superb mixture of both industrial and rural settings. For both authors, the images of the railways serving the west coast ports, like Helensburgh and Mallaig are gems, as they show how the railways linked with the unique coastal and inter-island ferries that were also a legend in their own right!

Above: In what is a truly atmospheric shot, we start this look at the Scottish Region, not on the west coast, but the east. There we find A2 Class 60532 *Blue Peter* alongside Class J37 0-6-0, 64602, at Dundee Tay Bridge shed (62B) on 6th June 1965. The A2 was one of those rebuilt with a double blast pipe and multiple valve regulator, whereas the J37 was to a North British Railway design by P W Reid from 1914. *Strathwood Library Collection* (E201)

Right: The 0-6-0 tender locomotive had a widespread application on the LNER system, and it was found in many different guises. This one, 65917, is a Class J38 0-6-0 that was designed by Nigel Gresley and introduced from 1926. The J38 had a boiler that was six inches longer than the J39, but had a smoke-box that was six inches shorter. Seven were however rebuilt with J39 boiler, including 65917 shown here at Fishcross with a goods from Dollar on 25th August 1967. *J R Beddows* (E186)

Top Left: For a variety of reasons, the British Railway Standard classes were not always liked by the crews who operated them. From most of the BR regions there came to be a less than satisfactory account of how different members of the 999-strong engine had failed to live up to expectations. Yet the Scottish crews are reported to have made the best of them, especially the Britannia and Clan class 4-6-2s. Less criticised, but still no favourite of many fitters, were the BR Standard Class 5MT two-cylinder 4-6-0 locomotives with Caprotti valve gear. This particular example, 73149, was built at Derby in 1957 and is seen here at Stirling on 10th June 1965. It is fitted with the BR1B type tender holding 4,725 gallons of water.
Peter Coton (B206)

Bottom Left: The Britannia class 7P6F Pacifics did some of their best work north of the Border, especially along the old Caledonian Main Line. It is on that railway, between Glasgow and Perth, where 70016 *Ariel* rattles along with a six coach train at Blackford on 10th June 1965. Despite its once busy status as a rural station, the facilities at Blackford were to suffer a dramatic downturn in traffic after World War II and the former Caledonian Railway station closed to passengers on 11th June 1956, although goods facilities lasted for a further 11 years before finally being removed on 11th September 1967. The engine pictured here was built at Crewe in 1951 and originally allocated to the Western Region.
Michael Beeton (B222)

Above: The ten members of the Clan Class 4-6-2s were rated as 6P5F locomotives and were allocated to Polmadie and the ex-Caledonian Railway depot of Carlisle Kingmoor. They weighed in at 6-tons 1-cwt lighter than the Britannia Class 4-6-2s, and had slightly smaller cylinders. A further build of 15 more Clans was however put on hold, and these were never built, although there are now proposals to build a new one *Hengist* for the heritage railway movement.

The engine seen here heading south after its descent from Beattock in May 1960, 72006 *Clan MacKenzie* was designed at Derby and out-shopped from Crewe in February 1952. At the time of its production it was estimated to have cost £21,283 11s 6d, but when it was withdrawn at Kingmoor in May 1965 it was sold to J.W. Williams for scrap for just £2,015. Note the Moffat branch just curving away to the right. *Trans Pennine Archive* (B186)

Above: Seen here shorn of its nameplates, yet still looking remarkably clean, Britannia 70031 *Byron* (then based at Carlisle Upperby (12B) rests at Carstairs (66E) on 7th June 1966. This shed had an interesting history after its shed code was changed from 64D on 18th June 1960s, and within three years it was classed as 'diesel only' in August 1963. It then closed completely the following month, only to re-open as a 'temporary steam depot' in December 1966. It closed to steam on 2nd February 1967 and then closed completely the following month and was thereafter only used as a stabling point for diesels and as a 'signing on point' for crews.

The Britannia also had an interesting history, after it was outshopped in November 1952. It was first of all allocated to Holyhead and worked on the Irish Mail express turns for a short while before being sent to Manchester Longsight early in 1953. Seven years later it was still at work in the Manchester District, transferring to Trafford Park in 1960. By 1962 it was at Aston and at Willesden a year later. At the start of 1965 it was at Crewe (North and South) and eventually went north to end its days at Carlisle (Upperby then Kingmoor) in 1966. It was withdrawn in November 1967 and scrapped at McWilliams of Shettlestone in March 1968. *Michael Beeton* (B236)

Below: The doyen of the Clan Class, 72000 *Clan Buchanan* is seen at Beattock with a Glasgow - Liverpool working in May 1960. This locomotive entered service in December 1951along with 72001 *Clan Cameron*, to be joined a month later by 72002 and 72003. In February 72004-5 were ready for traffic, with the latter engine being sent to Carlisle Kingmoor, which was then still a Scottish Region shed. The next four engines, 72006-9 also went to Kingmoor.

Ironically the first members of the class were all withdrawn in 1962 after just 11 years in service, and they were prematurely cut up at Darlington Works by February 1964 with *Clan Buchanan* having just 465,968 miles on the clock. Note that Beattock shed (66F) is just visible in the background of the view, this was also used as diesel stabling point after its official closure on 1st May 1967.
Trans Pennine Archive (B200)

Top Left: Concluding our study of BR Standard Class engines on the Scottish Region for the moment, we see 70009 *Alfred the Great* at Carstairs. This was originally an Eastern Region 4-6-2 and allocated to Norwich after it was built at Crewe in May 1951. It was loaned to the Southern Region (Nine Elms) in September 1951, but shortly returned to Norwich. As dieselisation later swept through East Anglia, it was put into store at March MPD before being transferred to Carlisle Kingmoor (12A) in December 1963. It would remain at work there the end of 1966 and was officially withdrawn in January 1967. It was sent north to McWilliams of Shettlestone in the spring of 1967 and handed over to the scrapmen in May of that year. It is seen here at Carstairs on 8th June 1966, by which time its nameplates have already been removed. *Peter Coton* (B241)

Bottom Left: One of the express locomotive classes more commonly associated with the Scottish Region was the A4 4-6-2 with its 8P6F power rating. Here we see the A4 that carries the name of its designer, 60007 *Sir Nigel Gresley,* at Buchanan Street Station in Glasgow on 8th June 1965 alongside a BR Standard Class 5 4-6-0 with Caprotti valve gear, 73152. Neither locomotive looks in pristine condition, and the station buildings also have an unkempt feel about them. This perhaps hardly surprising as the former Caledonian Railway station had lost its freight facilities in 1962 and would close completely in November 1966.
Peter Coton (E261)

Above: Other BR 'standard' classes to see widespread use in Scotland were the ex-WD Austerity 2-8-0s and 2-10-0s. Scottish crews made good use of locomotives like 90534 a WD 2-8-0 pictured at Alloa (North British station) on 29th June 1966. This station was renamed Alloa East in 1951 and closed to passengers on 7th June 1968, but freight lasted until the Summer of 1974.

The thriving port of Alloa was, over the years, served by no less than five stations; three of these were Caledonian, the last of which closed in 1885. The first station, Alloa Ferry of the Stirling & Dunfermline railway, closed as early as 1852 and as its name implies it linked with a small ferry across the Firth of Forth until it was superseded by a 1,600 foot bridge in October 1885. *Michael Beeton* (B280)

Above: Another of the WD 2-8-0s allocated to Scotland was 90386, which was formerly WD 78592 allocated to March but then served at Boulogne after the Allied invasion. She was of course Scottish by birth, being built by the North British Locomotive Co. in Glasgow to works number 25353 in 1944. It was therefore fitting that this engine would spend her last ten years in Scotland before being notionally allocated for one month to Sunderland (52G) in December 1966. However, as steam was hastily being cut back in the North Eastern Region at that time, it is generally believed she did not go south of the border again.

It is likely that 90386 remained at Dunfermline (62C), and then went to one of the Scottish Region's temporary dumps that began building up around sheds and junctions in this period. It was destined for Cowlairs Works for cutting after its official withdrawal date of 15th April 1967, but by that time the BR works had ceased this work, although ten others of the class had by then been handled by Cowlairs. It was therefore sold to the Motherwell Machinery & Scrap Co. of Wishaw in September 1967, the largest of the private scrapyards in Scotland.
Michael Beeton (B291)

Below: Not all the steam locomotives withdrawn from Scottish Region sheds in the 1950s and '60s went straight to the scrap line, indeed some continued to serve a useful purpose for quite a while after their 'working lives' had officially ended. Stationary boilers, steam heating units and so on provided some extra longevity for these engines, and thereby eked out their existence. A good example of this is pictured with 54476, seen here at Stirling in 1958 after its running days had come to an end.

This class of 4-4-0 was designed by W Pickersgill and based on an earlier design by J McIntosh. Like the WD 2-8-0 seen opposite, 54476 was also a North British Locomotive product, but other members of this once numerically strong class were built also by the Caledonian Railway's own workshops at St. Rollox and by Armstrong Whitworth. It was finally withdrawn in March 1960 and cut up at St. Rollox Works that July.
Trans Pennine Archive (M452)

Above: North of the Firth of Forth and South of the River Tay stands the ancient Kingdom of Fife, which has a very interestin history. However, in railway terms its history was predominantly associated with the North British Railway and its predecessor the Edinburgh & Northern Railway. The route to the towns of North East Scotland was its primary goal, for lucrative coal traffic was to be found in Fife, whilst the maritime ports of Dundee, Arbroath, Montrose and Aberdeen all offered rich pickings for the railways that could provide direct links to the main centres of population in either Edinburgh or Glasgow.

Yet the crossings of the Firth of Forth and the Firth of Tay presented a major obstacle. Once these two great rivers were bridged, the coalfields and fishing ports could be opened up for traffic, and some great engine sheds were established, including that at Thornton Junction (62A) near Weymss. On 13th August 1964 we see a Class J37 0-6-0, 64632, at the corrugated 'lighting shed', which was built for oiling up during the wartime blackout. Thornton Junction closed to steam on 5th June 1967, although diesels continued to be allocated there until July 1970.
Strathwood Library Collection (E94)

Top Right: The Caledonian Railway sought to provide its links to North East Scotland by way of a route through Stirling, Dunblane and Perth, throwing off (en-route) a branch line to Alloa and a long, winding cross-country line back to Oban and Ballachulish on the West Coast. Large locomotive depots were established at both Perth and Stirling, although Perth (63A) was the main shed, with sub-sheds at Aberfeldy, Blair Atholl and Crieff. Stirling South (63B) had a sub-shed many miles to the west at Killin on the side of Loch Tay. This was the scene towards the end of steam at Perth, as a Black 5 44998 stands with a North British 0-4-0 diesel shunter, D2725, on 17th August 1967. Both these locomotives are withdrawn and are 'stored' pending their removal to scrapyards. Note spare brick arches neatly labelled and piled, but most unlikely to be used again as steam is in its final retreat.
Michael Patterson (M461)

Bottom Right: A great feature about train spotting in Scotland was the fact that there were always examples of older designs to be found here during the 1960s. A good example of this is 64547, a J37 0-6-0 class that was introduced back in 1914 by the NBR. Although looking quite antiquated, they had a 5F power classification and were a superheated improvement on the Class J35s that Reid had brought out from 1906 onwards. This survivor was seen at Dundee Tay Bridge, with a rake of empty coal wagons on 24th September 1966. *Win Wall, Strathwood Library Collection* (E281)

Left: At the nearby Tay Bridge MPD (62B) on 25th August 1966, we capture 60813 a V2 Class 2-6-2 resting between duties. These versatile mixed traffic engines were a lifeline for the LNER during World War II, when they handled anything from humble freight trains to top link express workings on the East Coast Main Line. Note the engine's stove pipe chimney and smoke deflectors.
Peter Coton (E286)

Above: Moving north of Dundee on the old Caledonian Railway takes us next to Forfar MPD (63C) in September 1960. Here we see a withdrawn ex-Caledonian 0-4-4T, 55215 next to a refurbished Shell-BP oil tanker that is being used to fuel the replacement diesel shunters. It was withdrawn officially in October 1961 but had been stored since March that year. The loco was sent to Inverurie works in December and cut up in January 1962. *Trans Pennine Archive* (M460)

Left: Another Caledonian railway locomotive stored at Forfar in the summer of 1959 was 54503, a 4-4-0 that had been built by the North British Locomotive Co. at Glasgow in 1922. A member of the Caledonian 72 class, this was a Perth (63A) engine for many years, but was taken out of active service in 1958 along with many 4-4-0s around the country. It remained at Perth until March 1959 and was then placed in store at Forfar until January 1960 and was finally scrapped by Arnott Young at Old Kilpatrick the next month. *Trans Pennine Archive* (M453)

Above: Still very much alive, and seemingly the subject of a debate between the engine crews is 60919 a V2 class 2-6-2, which is seen at Falkirk Grahamstown on 9th April 1966. Falkirk was of course central to early plans to create a cross Scotland route, with the Forth & Clyde Canal, which opened in 1790, and the Union Canal that provided a link to Edinburgh that opened in 1822. In railway terms Falkirk's importance followed as a strategic junction on the North British Railway system. *Strathwood Library Collection* (E287)

Above: The vast numbers of redundant locomotives that were stored around Scotland in the early 1960s was quite significant, as the thrifty shed masters seemed reluctant to part with engines that might yet have some use. Coupled with this the BR works at Cowlairs, Inverurie, Kilmarnock and St. Rollox were working as best they could through a never-ending procession of un-wanted engines. As a consequence of supply exceeding the capacity, a series of small dumps began to be established around the Scottish Region, notably at Falkirk as mentioned previously.

Others were established at Thornton Junction, and also at Polmont (which we believe is shown here), before a larger dump was established alongside the docks at Bo'ness. At first these dumps were filled with the older pre-Grouped Scottish railway types, like the North British Railway Class C16 4-4-2T 67492, and the BR-built Class J72 0-6-0T, 69014, that is seen alongside. Note how the C16 has been carefully protected from the elements, with the chimney covered by canvas in the faint hope of a reprieve.
Trans Pennine Archive (E282)

Below: The plethora of Scottish sheds that were used to store redundant steam included another of the big depots in Fife, namely that at Dunfermline MPD (62C). It was a natural resting place for many engines being moved from the Edinburgh sheds to the works at Inverurie, however like Perth and Kittybrewster, it seemed to be mostly a transient point, with engines staying a few weeks or a month or so at the most. Its own 'redundant' engines tended to last a while longer, officially stored, and not as yet marked for disposal. This includes 65931 a J38 class 0-6-0 introduced by Gresley in 1926. It is seen at the shed on 28th August 1966, along with several other redundant North British 0-4-0 diesel shunters before being moved to Shipbreaking Industries at Faslane in January 1967. The shed closed to steam on 5th June 1967 before closing completely on 22nd September 1969. *J R Beddows* (E285)

Top Left: The Scottish allocation of A4 Class Pacifics was still very active in the early 1960s, and would remain so until the autumn of 1966. The class did however suffer the indignity of losing five of their members from Kings Cross (34A), 60003, 60014, 60028, 60030 and 60033 were all sent to Doncaster Works for disposal at the end of 1962. Four months later this was followed by 60013, 60015 and 60022 and the Eastern Region stud was in full retreat. The loss of A4s from Kings Cross, Gateshead and latterly New England meant that only 19 of the 'Streaks' were left at the end of 1963. Five were transferred to Scotland from the Eastern Region, and four were sent from the North Eastern Region shed at Gateshead (52A). By March 1964 the Scottish Region began to suffer its withdrawals too, and 60005 left Aberdeen Ferryhill (61B) for Campbell's yard in Airdrie. However, the reprieve afforded to the A4s by their transfer to the Scottish Region undoubtedly ensured that several of these impressive locomotives would go off into preservation. Here we see 60019 *Bittern* at Ferryhill (61B) on 1st June 1966.
Peter Coton (E270)

Bottom Left: One A4 destined to be spared the carnage (as it was earmarked for the National Collection), was the record-breaking 60022 *Mallard*. It is seen here at Edinburgh Waverley with the Aberdeen Flyer special on a miserable 2nd June 1962. Note how the curve of the handrail is a necessity rather than aesthetic.
Strathwood Library Collection (E279)

Above: The 'Road to the Isles' was always important to the economy of Scotland, and the creation of the North British Railway route to Fort William was therefore of major significance. Yet the territory that the railway would pass through was hardly alive with traffic, especially over Rannoch Moor. It was of course highly picturesque, and from the outset the railway was not slow to market the attractions found en-route.

The extension to Mallaig via the West Highland Railway offered even more scenic value, as the lonely line continued to the fishing port of Mallaig, from where the ferries sailed to the Isle of Skye. Seen awaiting its fate at the terminus of Mallaig, is K2 2-6-0 class, 61791 *Loch Laggan*, which was a sub-class of the K1 and was provided with side windows on the cab and a larger boiler.

Trans Pennine Archive (E269)

Left: The shed at Mallaig was a sub-shed of Fort William (65J), which in turn came under Glasgow Eastfield (65A). However, on 18th June 1960 Fort William was transferred from Stirling (63B) as a sub-shed and on that very day we see a B1 class 4-6-0, 61197, simmering gently in the sun. Note the electrification warning signs on the front of the engine, as the famous Glasgow 'Blue' trains were not to be so far away.
Frank Hornby (E275)

Above: It is the turn of a named B1, 61243 *Sir Harold Mitchell* to take us from Fort William back to the smoke of Glasgow on 18th June 1960. For the first part of the journey she will be piloted by a K1 class 2-6-0, 62052. The pair is seen here awaiting departure from Fort William on a part of the old formation that is now part of the town's by-pass. The B1 class was over 400 members strong, but of these just 58 were named!
Frank Hornby (E272)

Above: Even relatively busy junctions had a rural outlook in many parts of Scotland, including that at Lumphinans Central, where we see a B1 class 4-6-0, 61072, on 22nd August 1966. Like many engines that ventured into the Fife and Kinross coalfields, this was an engine from Dunfermline (62C), but in November it went to Dundee's Tay Bridge MPD (62B) and would last there to the end of its service life in June 1967.

An interesting aside about this junction was the fact that when the Kinross-shire Railway opened in 1860, four railway policemen (the early name for signalmen) were stationed here. This company's 6½ mile single-track line opened in June that year, running from the Edinburgh Perth & Dundee line at Lumphinans (some times spelt Lumphinnans) to a terminus at Kinross.

J R Beddows (E284)

Below: This view of 55227 at Kyle of Lochalsh in 1959 is truly a rural view, as it is at the end of one of Britain's most scenic railways - the old Highland Railway's road to the isles. For years this was one of the two major rail and ferry routes to Skye, and the line still remains today, albeit the road bridge to Skye has taken over much of the line's former traffic.

The 0-4-4T was a Caldeonian 439 class to a type introduced by McIntosh in 1900. In 1959 it was allocated to Inverness (60A), but sub-shedded to Kyle from where it was withdrawn in December 1961. It would be one of the relatively few locomotives that would travel south to the Inverurie Works, where it was scrapped in February 1962. *Win Wall, Strathwood Library Collection* (M456)

Above: The origins of Helensburgh date back to about 1600, but it did not become a town until 1776 when Sir Ian Colquhoun of Luss planned a new spa resort and named it after his wife, Helen. Helensburgh later became associated with the world's first seagoing steamship, after Henry Bell built the *Comet* to bring customers from Glasgow to his wife's hotel. The Glasgow, Dumbarton & Helensburgh Railway opened in 1858, terminating at Helensburgh Central, where we see a Gresley-designed Class V1 2-6-2T, 67629, under the impressive Victorian glass canopies.
Trans Pennine Archive (E289)

Right: After 1858 a popular practice soon developed, whereby Glaswegians would use the railway trains and steamers to take a circular tour to Helensburgh. As a result the railway was extended to a new pier that was built to serve the demand for the steamer services, including to destinations on the Clyde, Loch Long and beyond. With the pier in the background, we see another V1, 67655, alongside 67474 a C15 Class 4-4-2T. This was one of the two remaining survivors of the class and allocated to Glasgow Eastfield (65A) when this picture was taken in June 1959.
Trans Pennine Archive (E262)

Top Left: Scotland is associated worldwide for its renowned pipes and drums, but the selection of drums shown in this series of pictures has an entirely different meaning! The drums concerned are of the variety that contains oil, that most vital fluid that has provided lubricants for all manner of moving machinery. It may not be widely appreciated just how much oil a working railway consumes, but many shed or depot pictures often contain views of oil drums stacked away in the odd corner. This is just one example, as we see a J36 Class 0-6-0, 65288, to an 1888 design by M Holmes for the North British Railway. Along with a collection of Shell oil drums, it sits basking in the watery sunlight at Dunfermline MPD (62C) on 14th January 1967.
J R Beddows (E277)

Bottom Left: More Shell Oil drums are obvious at Ayr MPD (67C) on 6th June 1966. However, perhaps engine 42789 might have expected to be looking for Castrol Oil instead. If so, this would be because this Hughes 'Crab' 2-6-0 engine was built at Crewe Works in 1927 by the LMS as their 13089 and originally fitted with 'Wakefield' Lubricators. The connection between Castrol and the name Wakefield being that the magnate Lord (Sir Charles) Wakefield owned the oil company. His connections with the world of transport includes many motor sport events, the Ravenglass & Eskdale Railway, Ullswater Steamers and the pioneering solo flight that Amy Johnson undertook between England and Australia to name but a few!
J R Beddows (M459)

Top Right: Yet more Shell drums are pictured at the former NBR shed at Dunfermline (62C), along with a cache of BP and Castrol drums on 28th June 1966 as 61350 and 90229 are captured 'on shed'. The first of these engines is a B1 Class 4-6-0, the other an ex-War Department 2-8-0. Built in 1943 it was initially allocated to Carlisle Kingmoor, an ex-Caledonian Railway shed before it saw service in Belgium after the Allies liberated that country. When WD 77314 was withdrawn from overseas service, the Ministry of Supply 8F was initially allocated to the busy South Yorkshire coalfields and based at Mexborough (41F). Much later on it returned to Scotland, where the class saw widespread use. It would also meet its end in Scotland, for following withdrawal in September 1966 it was sold to J McWilliams yard at Shettleston in December.
J R Beddows (B340)

Bottom Right: Looking like its boiler could do with a wipe from an oily rag, this pure bred Stanier Black 5 4-6-0, 44973, is seen at a former Caledonian Railway shed. This is Carstairs (64D), which was a convenient shed for those that bothered to get off at the junction station (where Glasgow and Edinburgh portions of WCML trains would split) and then gain access via a footbridge. It is a pity that this doesn't seem to have been a favourite shed for too many photographers, as these hard-working engines could always be found here; as per the example of the soot-encrusted Black 5 on 3rd June 1965.
Strathwood Library Collection (M80)

Top Left: Another grimy engine is seen with B1 Class 4-6-0, 61347, pictured at Balgownie on 23rd August 1966. This engine was withdrawn from Thornton Junction (62A) but then moved north to a small dump at Dundee Tay Bridge (63B) between April and August 1967. It finally moved to McLellans at Langloan for disposal in September. It is pictured in slightly happier days with a train of pallet vans, and passing a British Railways Signalling & Telegraph Department Series I Land Rover in the field alongside.
J R Beddows (E273)

Bottom Left: Not too far south from Thornton Junction, another ex-NBR shed was found at Dunfermline (62C). It is there that we see BR Standard Class 4, 76110, in what we believe to be a 1965 picture. This engine was built at Doncaster in 1957, as part of a batch of 15 such engines for the Scottish Region. Note the narrow gauge hopper wagons used in locomotive service at the Motive Power Depot.
Len Smith (B283)

Right: The same engine has found its way east to Alloa on 25th August 1966, where it is seen on a permanent way train. Originally shedded at Thornton Junction (62A) it became a Dunfermline MPD (62C) engine from May 1960 but was withdrawn prematurely at the end of 1966. It was stored at Dunfermline until March 1967, but at ten years old it was decreed to be of no further use. It was broken up by Shipbreaking Industries at Faslane in April 1967.
J R Beddows (B290)

Above: The 4-4-0 design was for many years the mainstay of British locomotive practice, but as a consequence of the Modernisation it was considered as having no future on British Railways. One of the longer lasting designs to this wheel arrangement was Gresley's D49 Class dating from 1927, and 59 of these were still active in 1959. This one, 62711 *Dumbartonshire* is seen at Edinburgh St Margarets (64A) on 12th June 1960.
Frank Hornby (E269)

Right: One 4-4-0 class that was down to an unlucky 13 by 1959 was Reid's North British D30 introduced in 1912. One of the more popular members of the class, at least with young enthusiasts of the day was 62418 *The Pirate*, which is seen here on pilot duties at Thornton Junction (62A) in May 1959. It was withdrawn that August and then stored at the shed before going to Arnott Young's scrapyard at Old Kilpatrick in early 1960.
Trans Pennine Archive (E290)

Above: The D30 Class, and other aspects of the North British Railway had been given names of links with the celebrated 'Waverley Novels' by Sir Walter Scot. Whilst predominantly associated with the Border Counties, the NBR found it to be good publicity to widen their association over much of their territory, and perhaps the best example of this would be the naming of their principle station in Scotland's Capital as Edinburgh Waverley, and it is here we visit for our next picture.

On a rainy 5th May 1965, we see a clean looking A3 60052 *Prince Palatine*, complete with cab-side warning stripe showing that this engine must not work south of Crewe under the overhead electric lines. This St. Margarets-based engine would work down the former NBR Waverley line through the Border Counties to Carlisle on an enthusiast's special; note the German Federal Railway pattern smoke deflectors that are fitted to the Gresley designed A3.
Strathwood Library Collection (E276)

Top Right: Although Scotland could boast its share of prestigious steam locomotives, particularly on the Aberdeen - Perth - Glasgow service, as well as the Glasgow - Edinburgh express passenger trains. Yet elsewhere the railway scene could be quite antiquated, and locomotive practice still carried forward many features that would have been familiar with Victorian railway enthusiasts. The engine shed at St. Margarets (64A) was a place of remarkable contrasts in the mid-1960s, with a host of different locomotive types to be seen, with the very latest diesel types alongside BR Standards, LNER locomotives, and engines from the pre-Grouped era. On 4th June 1963 we see A3 60052 *Prince Palatine* by the shed's turntable with A4 60034 *Lord Faringdon*.
Peter Cotton (E256)

Bottom Right: An antiquated engine with solid buffers is to be seen in this photograph of 68338 dating from 1959. This J88 Class 0-6-0T was at the time based at Edinburgh St Margarets (64A), but commonly worked on the docks at Leith. It was to a North British Railway design dating from 1905, and was provided with an especially short wheel base to allow it to work on railway systems with sharp curves. It was therefore found in dockyards, locomotive or wagon works and industrial sidings. As most of the J88's work involved shunting, they were fitted with dumb buffers to avoid buffer lock, and as late as 1959 no less than 26 of them were still on the stock list.
Trans Pennine Archive (E263)

Above: Another member of the J88 Class with dumb (unsprung) buffers was 68342 and it was also a St Margarets - based engine. It is seen on that shed, surrounded by its larger stablemates on 12th June 1960. St. Margarets was a 30 minutes walk from Waverley according to Ian Allan Shed Directories, the shed was on both sides of the line and carried a warning to be careful crossing the line! St Margarets was an indirect victim of the BRB decree to end haulage of all passenger trains by steam locomotives.

The Scottish Region modernisation was assisted by the arrival of ex-ER Class 24s from Finsbury Park and ex-WR Class 37s from Cardiff. This finally allowed the dieselisation of the Edinburgh - Carstairs services, whilst on the Waverley route return workings to Carlisle and locals trips to Hawick saw the Class 24s taking over diagrams planned for the Clayton and Class 26 diesels; as a result Waverley became less and less frequented by steam engines.
Frank Hornby (E259)

Below: Also found at St Margarets 12th June 1960, was Y9 Class 0-4-0ST, 68119, yet another Victorian survivor. Dating from the Holmes North British design of 1882, this tiny engine weighed in at a little under 28-tons, but some (like 68119) were permanently paired to a little wooden tender or match truck that weighed 6-tons.

The tender (which also doubled as a shunter's truck) is well illustrated in this view, but note also the engine's stovepipe chimney showing signs of exertion. As for St. Margarets MPD, it closed to steam in December 1966 and Edinburgh's premier shed did not last very long thereafter.
Frank Hornby (E231)

Above: The transition for steam to diesel power is well illustrated by yet another picture of a Class Y9 0-4-0ST, 68104 (this time not one of those paired to a wooden tender), as it rests in front of D3733. This member of the BR 0-6-0 Diesel Shunter class (which would later be known as a Class 08) was introduced in 1959 and allocated to St. Margarets on 2nd April that year. These weighed in at 47-tons, and were thus almost 20 tons heavier than the North British-designed Y9.
Trans Pennine Archive (E292)

Right: Returning to St.Margarets on 28th June 1966, we see a 'withdrawn to traffic' locomotive eking out its final days, as J36 Class 0-6-0 65234 acts as stationary boiler for the shed. This was yet another Victorian design, dating from 1888 when Holmes introduced them as mixed traffic engines on the North British Railway. After World War I some were given names to commemorate famous generals or battles, but the end of the 1950s just 86 of these old soldiers were left and many of them were already in store.
Frank Hornby (E221)

Above: The process of cascading engines from the Eastern and North Eastern regions into Scotland during the 1960s saw some well known engines operating in Scotland. Arguably one of the better known Scottish engines of the day, because of its frequent appearances on the BBC's childrens' programme of the same name was A2 Class 60532 *Blue Peter*, which is pictured as it stops for water at Forfar on the former Caledonian Railway inland route from Perth to Aberdeen. A victim of Beeching, this line closed completely in September 1967, although the attractive branches that diverged from this line to Alyth, Blairgowrie and Kirriemuir had already each been robbed of their passenger services in 1951, 1955 and 1952 respectively. Note the fire devil at the base of the water column, a reminder that winter was never far away in Eastern Scotland! *Strathwood Library Collection* (E80)

Below: Anyone who was a youngster in the late 1950s or early 1960s will remember the original Blue Peter presenter Christopher Trace. He won the job before the programme went on air in 1958 when he bonded with the producer John Hunter Blair over their love of trains. Whilst being interviewed, Trace enthusiastically played with a OO gauge layout in Hunter Blair's office. The Blue Peter train set would become a regular feature of the series, and was often brought out of retirement long after Trace's departure.

Naturally, a regular 'star' of the show was the A2 Class, 60532 *Blue Peter* even though the programme name had more to do with maritime heritage. Though 60532 had become one of the last few Pacifics in Scotland, it was requested for the use of a large number of specials right around the country, including trips that took it on to the Southern. It is seen here at Aberdeen Ferryhill (61B) on 16th June 1966.

Strathwood Library Collection (E280)

Left: The transfer of the A4s to the Scottish Region saw many enthusiasts travelling north to watch locomotives like 60004 *William Whitelaw* working their last days. Not surprisingly they would also be requested to head many enthusiast specials as, for example, this one which we believe is seen at Aberdeen in 1966; just look at the number of people with cameras in this view.
Trans-Pennine Archive (E296)

Above: The steam enthusiasts preferred motive power on the Aberdeen runs was 60019 *Bittern*, which is seen here at Perth. Although this was the so-called Indian Summer of the A4s it was not always blessed with sunny days for cameramen. Perth was a Caledonian Railway station and a hub for several routes, but the lines north to the highlands were dieselised early in the 1960s.
J.R. Beddows (E278)

Top Left: Another of the great classes to be seen working in Scotland from the 1930s onwards were the LMS Coronation 4-6-2s introduced by Sir William Stanier in 1937. However, photographs of these great engines are considerably rarer than the A4, even though they were progressively withdrawn from 1962 onwards. In December that year Polmadie (66A) lost three of its allocation, as 46227, 46231 and 46232 (which had escaped a Nazi bomb at Berkhampstead in 1940) were all sent to Crewe for scrapping. Here we see 46230 Duchess of Buccleuch (another Crewe victim) as it waits to head south from Glasgow Central in 1958. This loco was also withdrawn at the end of 1962 but it had covered very little mileage in her last year of BR service, and this indicated it had spent a lot of time in store. There was some delay in making the decision to cut them up, and she was kept at Crewe Works until the autumn of 1963 when it was finally dismantled. *Trans-Pennine Archive* (M449)

Bottom Left: Whereas the crew of the 'Duchess' appear to be waiting idly for their journey to start, there is quite a lot of activity on the footplate of Jubilee Class 4-6-0 45697 *Achilles* as she barks out of Beattock in September 1959. Note the Fowler style of tender, which is fitted with the extra rails to increase capacity and prevent stray cobs of coal from rolling off what was not always a smooth-riding loco! It is a warm day and the crew have the cab roof shutter open to let in more air and light. *Trans-Pennine Archive* (M440)

Above: Another Stanier design to be found in many parts of Scotland was the Black 5 4-6-0, an example of which (44720) is seen at Stirling (by then 65J) on 7th June 1966. The 4-6-0 looks remarkably smart with fresh paint evident on both the smokebox door and buffer beam, despite this being the last week of steam at this shed. Furthermore, as we see the replacements are already here.The question, as then unanswered was, would the North British Class 21 diesels cope with the undulating road to Aberdeen? History shows that the answer was an unequivocal no!

Such were the problems with this fleet that in early 1963 D6123 was dispatched to Davey Paxman's works in Colchester where a 'Ventura' engine was fitted. This Bo-Bo was then tested in Scotland and a decision was taken that this power unit was more reliable than the original type, and it culminated in a fleet of 20 locos being re-engined. Under the National Traction Plan the re-engined examples were permitted to carry on working in Scotland, remaining active until late 1971. Even so it was a short service life and they were all sold for scrap. *J.R. Beddows* (M433)

Left: Another 0-6-0 to be found in Scotland was Gresley's J38 Class, which had been first introduced by the LNER in 1926. It weighed in at 58-tons 19-cwt, whilst the tender was 44-tons 4-cwt, and had a tractive effort of 28,415lbs. Here we see another example, 65925, at Lumphinans East Junction on 22nd August 1966. The J38s were normally overhauled at Cowlairs Works, and many of them were cut up there, but the last two members of the class lasted until April 1967.

J.R. Beddows (E239)

Above: Although diesel traction was by then making inroads into the Scottish Region's dwindling traffic, steam would continue to be evident well into 1967. Here we see a J37 Class 0-6-0, 64620, at Touch Junction with a down goods train. This was a long-term Dundee Tay Bridge (62B) engine and it would remain there until it was withdrawn in April 1967. Before long the engine and tender would become a lifeless 95.5-ton lump of scrap to be cut up by the Motherwell Machinery & Scrap Co. at Wishaw.

J.R. Beddows (E252)

Above: One of the most successful locomotives to appear in Scotland were the Thompson B1 Class 4-6-0s which, for many enthusiasts, rivalled the LMS Black 5. The general assumption by many was that the B1 was inferior to its contemporaries, but the 1948 Locomotive Exchanges did not prove this. The two classes were of course very similar in boiler pressure, weight and tractive effort and the main differences were the driving wheel diameter and the boiler. The LMS boiler was of course based on the GWR 's taper boiler and could be fired anyhow, whereas the B1's boiler was constructed during the war years when a simpler construction was necessary.

Nevertheless the B1 had a good boiler when properly fired and the Scottish crews undoubtedly got the knack of doing this well. The driving wheels of the B1, at 6ft 2in diameter, made them more suitable to passenger work, but they were equally at home on freight turns, such as that seen here with 61102. This was a long time resident of Dundee, where she is doing a little shunting on 25th August 1966. Like many Scottish steam locos, she was withdrawn the following April. The B1 lingered around for another four months before being shunted off to McLellans at Langloan who had cut her up by September 1967.
Peter Coton (E220)

Below: We have mentioned that the Scottish Region sheds did particularly well with a number of classes of locomotives, but this is particularly noted with the BR Standards. One of the contributing factors was the high quality of water to be found throughout the region, and this imparted longer life to the boilers and less 'furring up' of the tubes and valves. This remarkable fact was noted in a number of official reports, as it became apparent that those Scottish-based engines did not require 'shopping' for boiler work as frequently as those based on other regions. Conversley the region's rougher track accounted for the Scottish Britannias having a low mileage between other works' visits. Here 9F 2-10-0, 92015, makes a welcome appearance at St. Rollox (65B). These behemoths were rarely seen in Scotland, with only a small number of turns from Carlisle bringing them up in daylight hours. Seen on 18th August 1964, she wears her Kingmoor (12A) shed-plate. St. Rollox was another ex-Caledonian shed, but it was a couple of miles from Glasgow Buchannan Street station and was a 40-minute walk, and this factor sadly seems to have put off many would-be photographers!
Strathwood Library Collection (B50)

Above: Here BR Standard Class 4MT 2-6-0 76098 is seen at Ayr MPD (67C). It was allocated here along with 76001, and 76096, this was a member of the third batch for Scotland. It was built at the former L&YR works at Horwich in 1957. Her life was to be a short one, and after Ayr MPD closed to steam in December 1966, she went north to Glasgow but little work was available. By May 1967 76098 was reduced to being a stationary boiler at Eastfield until February 1968. Ward's of Inverkeithing made a bid for the engine and their cutters had reduced the engine to scrap by March, 1967.
Len Smith (B279)

Right: The perversity that saw engines that had a 50-year projected life span being cut up after less than ten years service also claimed older, but nevertheless engines that had still not completed half of their expected service lives. A classic example is WD 2-8-0 90041. Seen near Alloa on 1st July 1966, this long-term resident of Aberdeen Ferryhill (61B) was withdrawn in December 1966. It was dumped at Dunfermline (62C) for three months and was handed over to J. McWilliams of Shettleston to carry out the last rites in April.
Michael Beeton (B77)

Top Left: Another short-lived waste of taxpayers' money, was Britannia class 4-6-2 70005, which was built at Crewe early in 1951. It was allocated to Stratford on the Eastern Region in April 1951, but put in to store that October, pending transfer to the London Midland Region and Rugby in December. In 1952 it spent some time at Rugby Test Station and was transferred back to Stratford in 1959. It went to Norwich at the end of that summer, and stored at March for two months in early 1963. Later that year it was allocated to both Crewe South and Stockport Edgely Park, and then put into store at Willesden from September to December. Out of store it went to Aston, and then had a final stint at Carlisle Kingmoor. Unloved and unwanted, the erstwhile *John Milton* has lost its nameplates in this scene captured south of Stirling on 8th June 1965. Even so it is hardly being taxed with its train just being comprised of a MkI Kitchen Car and 21-ton brake van.
Michael Beeton (B113)

Bottom Left: Another very short train is seen behind this Doncaster-built BR Standard 4-6-0. On 1st June 1966 Class 5MT 73100 has charge of the District Inspector's saloon as it pulls away from Perth Station. Sadly many workings such as this would have been taken as a result of the edict to reduce the overall size of the BR network that followed *The Reshaping of British Railways* report by Dr. Richard Beeching. It is also sad to relate that many of the old inspection saloons would not outlast steam either.
Peter Coton (B218)

Above: As stated earlier, many of the LNER B1 Class engines were embellished with nameplates, but this Eastfield (65A) example, sizzling away at a very damp looking Ayr, is one of the later and un-named examples. Ayr was long associated with holiday traffic heading south-west from Clydeside, and also with steamer crossings to the Isle Of Arran. The Glasgow & Ayr was planned as early as 1836, and concurrently promoted with the Glasgow Paisley & Greenock Rly. The two companies decided that the seven miles of line between Glasgow and Paisley would be owned and worked jointly. The section between Glasgow and Ayr was opened in 1839-40, whilst the eight mile branch from Dalry to Kilmarnock opened in 1843.

The project had also become involved in the struggle between the two projected routes from Glasgow to Carlisle. One of these, the route via Nithsdale and Dumfries, would eventually become the Glasgow & South Western route, whilst the other via the Upper Clyde Valley and Annandale would become the Caledonian Railway. The line promoted by the Glasgow Dumfries and Carlisle company was intended to run from Carlisle to Cumnock, where it would join an extension of the Ayr route. Note the rams leg cast ends to the platform seats at Ayr, with the B1 behind as it stopped under the ornate but compact canopy on 9th April 1966 so that the crew can keep dry.
Strathwood Library Collection (E86)

Above: We have visited Thornton Junction earlier in this book, and we return there in this view that dates from May 1959. Again we see another ex-LNER 4-4-0 at work in Scotland, as D49/2 'Hunt' Class 62744 *The Holderness* shows the cast brass fox embellishment above its nameplates. The picture also shows the Lentz rotary poppet valves driven by cams on the cylinders that were introduced on the D49/2s introduced in 1928. A second batch of D49/2s were fitted with Reidinger Rotary valves by BR in 1949.

Three different types of tenders were to be found on the D49s, and 62744 boasts the heavier (52-ton) LNER type. At the start of 1959 there were 30 D49/1s and 29 D49/2s still in service, but once the withdrawals started they would go fast. This one ended her service career at Hawick (64G) on the Waverley route in December of 1960, and after a short period in store at St. Margarets she went to join others of her class to be broken by Cowlairs Works in April 1961.
Trans-Pennine Archive (E271)

Above: The demise of the 4-4-0 in Scotland was hastened by the arrival of the new BR Standards, such as the Class 5MT 4-6-0 that had been introduced in 1951. In 1956 the BR workshops began to build a variant of this class with Caprotti valve gear, and a number of these were allocated to Scottish Region depots. The valve gear can be seen in some detail with this shot of 73152, then based at St. Rollox (65B) as it rests at Buchannan Street in Glasgow before it sets out from Glasgow on a run north.

One suspects that the taller fireman will be bending his back feeding the box on the journey as well as enduring the draughts that plagued these locos. As a consequence of the design they suffered badly with wind turbulence around the tender and the front of the cab. Although these engines were designed at 'The Plant' in Doncaster, it is quite obvious that wind tunnel testing was not really thought of as part of the design evaluation process for this class! *Peter Coton* (B230)

Left: Wind was a big problem for Scotland's first major estuarial crossing, that over the Firth of Tay. For example, the under-estimation of likely wind speeds by the Astronomer Royal lulled Thomas Bouch into a false sense of security when he designed his Tay Bridge. The pressures that the wind placed upon the great structure were never fully examined by the Board of Enquiry after the disaster on 28th December 1879, but it was so severe that the signalman at Wormit (pictured here), had to crawl on all-fours to get back to his box after giving a token to the driver of NBR 224 the ill-fated 4-4-0 that fell from the bridge with its train and claimed 75 lives when it plunged into the water below. *Michael Beeton* (E257)

Above: The remains of Bouch's bridge can be seen in the first of these two views taken on 9th June 1965 as a Class J37 0-6-0 64547 has just brought a few wagons off the bridge and onto the Tayport line at Wormit. The station was again the scene of another disaster on 25th May 1955, when a Class 5MT locomotive went around the curve at about 50mph, despite there being a 25mph speed limit. It derailed as a result, killing three and injuring 40. By way of contrast the Dundee Tay Bridge J37 seen here had a long and happy life. Along with 64569 it was the last survivor of the class when withdrawn in December 1966; the pair were finally taken to McWilliams of Shettleston for disposal in April 1967. *Michael Beeton* (E258)

Above: *As a final view we present another pair of J37s, 64570 and 64618, as they are seen awaiting their passengers for an enthusiasts special tour at Edinburgh Waverley on 25th June 1965.*
Strathwood Library Collection (E91)

EVERY PICTURE is worth a thousand words, or so they say, and thanks to the combined talents of photographers who have supplied material to both the Strathwood and Trans-Pennine archives, we have a lot to say in future volumes. Of course it would not have been possible to tell this story without the kind co-operation of the contributors named in the credits shown in this book. To those and all those who captured British Railways In Colour, we say a massive thank you! However mere words are never enough, and we hope that the ongoing series will provide a testimony to their far-sighted work.

In conclusion, can we offer a reminder that all of these published shots are available to purchase as superb duplicate slide copies direct from Strathwood. The code number at the end of each slide indicates its catalogue number, and also the name of the photographer whose work we felt warranted inclusion.

To get your copy of the extensive catalogue listing of these and many thousands of other shots available in fabulous colour, please send £5.00 to: -

Strathwood Limited
Kirkland House, Bruce Street, Whithorn.
Dumfries & Galloway DG8 8PY

Or visit the websites: -
www.strathwood.com or www.railwayslide.co.uk.

In return we will send the collector's catalogue, complete with sample slide, post free to UK addresses (overseas add £2.50).